Paleo: Instant Pot

The Ultimate Paleo Pressure Cooker Cookbook

Andrew Westbrook

Kaveman Cooking Publishing

informational purposes solely, and is universal as so. The presentation of the information is without contract or any type of guarantee assurance.

The trademarks that are used are without any consent, and the publication of the trademark is without permission or backing by the trademark owner. All trademarks and brands within this book are for clarifying purposes only and are the owned by the owners themselves, not affiliated with this document.

The material on this book is for informational purposes only. As each individual situation is unique, you should use proper discretion, in consultation with a health care practitioner, before undertaking the protocols, diet, exercises, techniques, training methods, or otherwise described herein. The author and publisher expressly disclaim responsibility for any adverse effects that may result from the use or application of the information contained herein.

Table of Contents

Desserts and Snacks 93

Introduction

So, you want to get started on the Paleo diet? Very nice decision! This book is here to help you get acquainted with the diet and to aid you as you venture forth in a possibly life changing experience.

Like all diets, the Paleo diet will not be a simple one to follow at first, but after you understand some of the ins and outs of the diet, it will become second-nature to you. It's not one of the phony "cure-all" diets you see on television or in magazine ads. It's hard to compare the Paleo diet with other diets out there simply because of the fact that it's more of a lifestyle than a modern-day diet.

Nevertheless, this diet and lifestyle change is a tough undertaking and will require patience and plenty of self-discipline (trust me, if you think that donut is tempting now, it will be like the forbidden fruit once you start the Paleo diet). Everyone is capable of reaping the benefits of this lifestyle change if they put in the effort. Before we go any further, some pressure cooker tips are on order, so let's get to it.

Do you own a pressure cooker? If so, no doubt you're as big a fan of it as I am. However, you might not be fully aware of the extent of a pressure cooker's abilities. You know how sometimes you get a new phone or computer and only learn to use their most basic functions? Same deal with a pressure cooker. Basic functions are great, but it can do so much more! There's a whole pressure cooker world beyond dinner stews. Delicious breakfasts, lunches, desserts; you name it, a pressure cooker probably has the capacity to create it easily in under an hour. So pull up a seat and let's take a close look at what this kitchen marvel can do for your life—and for your stomach.

I would suggest that you go over the manufacturer's guide to your own pressure cooker. Although I can lay out some general guidelines here, the manufacturer's guide for your specific pressure cooker will detail the exact ins and outs of your own pressure cooker. If the pressure cooker has been handed down to you, or you think you may not have the physical copy of the manufacturer's guide to your pressure cooker, there's really no need to worry. That's because you can simply search for your particular model online, and there may be an electronic version that you can go over. I know that reading an instruction manual may not seem like the most exciting way to spend your time (or maybe you're the type who likes to read instruction manuals, and if so, all the power to you!), but reading the guide will lay out additional pointers and how to's to get you started.

BEGINNER'S LOOK AT THE PRESSURE COOKER

How does a pressure cooker work? Basically, the lid creates a vacuum-sealed environment which traps steam inside the pressure cooker. As the level of steam rises, so does the pressure. Any substance in the pressure cooker, be it meat, soup, a casserole, etc., is then boiled or simmered, depending on the temperature you select, and is simultaneously infused with flavor. However, if you *weren't* using the pressure cooker, it would take twice as long to achieve the same effect. The pressure cooker is an amazing time saver, but unlike many shortcuts, this one doesn't cut corners in a way that negatively impacts the finished product. It will keep flavor intact and allow you more freedom to carry on with your day.

WHY USE A PRESSURE COOKER?

The following is a very short list of some great reasons to invest in an electric pressure cooker. No doubt, after you start using one regularly, you'll be inventing your own list, and the list will only keep growing from there.

- **EASY WAY TO PREPARE FOOD**—Unlike the earlier pressure cooker incarnations, electric ones have timers that you can set, allowing for maximum cooking convenience. Beyond the standard settings such as high, medium, and low, you don't need to worry about temperature or pressure. Unlike a stove, the pressure cooker does it all for you, and much more safely, too. This means that you will no longer have to be constantly checking in on your meal every few seconds. Once you've installed your pressure cooker in its designated spot and discovered how useful it is, it's likely that you'll always keep it at the ready for the next quick meal simply because of its convenience.

- **THE FASTER, THE BETTER**—Let's face it, our lives are busy. No one needs to tell you that (although I just did). Cooking meals in the oven can take hours and cooking on the stove requires a wary eye to keep dishes from overcooking. Pressure cookers can reduce cooking times by up to 2/3rds. When it might have taken 24 hours before to make a pot of beans, a pressure cooker makes the task so time-efficient that you'll no longer have to worry about watching the stove for hours on end.

- **DELICIOUS *CAN ALSO* MEAN NUTRITIOUS**—Remember the days of boiling food (like chicken) for hours on end? Boiling literally washes away key nutrients, whereas pressure cooking locks in all those necessary minerals and vitamins. This leaves you wanting to use your pressure cooker more often because of the additional health benefits that are available by following this style of cooking.

- **FEWER DISHES TO CLEAN**—Throw all your ingredients into the pressure cooker and lock the lid: It's the best version of a one pot meal you've ever made. When it's finished cooking, the only dishes will be the pot and the plates (which will undoubtedly have been licked clean because of how great the recipes in this book will taste!)

A BASIC HOW-TO FOR THE PRESSURE COOKER

You should be warned about one thing in particular. Although using a pressure cooker looks easy and sounds easy, that's because using a pressure cooker *is* easy. However, there's really only one major rule to follow, but that's one that can't be broken: Don't open that pot! You'll be tempted to, because you may have become so accustomed to stir things on the stove or check dishes in the oven every few minutes to make sure nothing burns. But unlocking the pressure cooker lid disrupts the steam environment and can affect your recipe, most of the time negatively. For maximum (and positive) results, follow the "no looking" rule. Simply resist the urge to constantly check up on your meal.

If you think you're now ready to begin your exciting foray into the Paleo lifestyle, go ahead and turn the page and, please, enjoy the introduction to the Paleo diet!

Chapter 1: What Exactly is the Paleo Diet?

In short, the entire purpose of the Paleo diet is to revert our eating habits back to our ancestors' way of eating -- in that, you'll focus your eating habits around what our cavemen ancestors ate. Now, that doesn't mean you have to invent the time machine and hunt mammoths! It simply means that a lot of the foods we eat today -- foods that were not available to our cavemen ancestors -- are off the table (no pun intended).

A lot of your "typical" diets include something about not eating sugars or fats or processed foods. While all of these shouldn't be indulged in every day, it's not as simple as cutting the fat off your steak for dinner. However, anything processed is definitely off limits (which means most things packed with preservatives, anything that requires a lot of processing to create, and of course all those sugary sweets).

So, what does that leave you to eat, aspiring Paleo dieters? Well, think back to the days of hunting and gathering. If you keep that in mind, you'll have an easy little cheat sheet to help you remember what you can eat while abiding by the Paleo lifestyle: Anything that our ancestors could have hunted or gathered.

This basically narrows your food down to two large groups of food: food you could hunt and food you could gather (after all, your ancestors *were* hunter-gatherers). While this may seem limiting when you think about all of the different foods you won't be able to enjoy any longer, the Paleo diet is actually far less limiting than, say, any other calorie-counting diet plan.

You may be wondering how exactly that's possible. Well, the Paleo diet does not place an emphasis on calorie intake (as many diets do), but rather focuses on the type of food that one ingests. The Paleo diet limits the food you eat (and therefore your caloric intake) to foods that are attainable through those two methods I mentioned earlier: Hunting and gathering. As you can imagine, many foods with an excessively high calorie count probably aren't found in nature –

you're not going to find a sugar-laden chocolate bar roaming around in the woods!

Limiting the food you eat to these naturally occurring plants and animals will naturally limit the amount of calories you ingest in a given day, which means another piece of good news for you: No more calorie calculations or counting, unless you're inclined to do so! Put your notebooks and smartphone apps away. The Paleo diet is designed to, essentially, count calories for you so you don't have to even think about it. After all, why should you worry about the exact amount of energy you put in your body if you know you're eating healthy and natural foods? For those who are interested, though, this book has comprehensive nutritional information for each recipe, which will be helpful if you're targeting certain macronutrient ratios.

At this point, there are usually one or two people that become skeptical of the Paleo diet and its seemingly easy set of rules. The Paleo diet is a very legitimate diet and, like any other diet out there, is not that easy.

Don't be worried about the difficulty of the diet. All diets require dedication, a bit of effort, and some time before the benefits start to show, but the Paleo diet is designed in order to make it as simple as possible: just follow the healthy rules it provides, and watch both losing weight and maintaining a healthy body become as easy as pie!

The next question that might be on your mind is something along the lines of "haven't humans evolved since our cavemen ancestors? How do we stay as fit as them if I can pick up three boxes of packaged frozen dinners from the store down the street?" While it's true that we are biologically different from our ancestors to some degree, it's equally as true that our ancestors didn't have the luxury of stores to drive to and pick up pounds and pounds of food. Nor did they have packaged frozen dinners, so avoid those as well.

Our ancestors relied on going out into the wild and finding food to survive. Mix their constant exercise that came from physically searching for their next meal with their diet consisting of all-natural meats and fruits, and you've got one healthy lifestyle.

This doesn't mean you should go out and hunt deer in the park a few blocks away with nothing but your hand-whittled spear and a loin cloth, but it does mean you should focus on getting mild to average levels of exercise throughout your week while watching the food you eat. Like I said, the Paleo diet is like many other diets in a lot of ways, but easier.

Chapter 2: The Origins of the Paleo Diet

What's this? A history lesson in a Paleo book? You better believe it! It's important to know a short history of the diet before diving in head first. Understanding where, why, and how the Paleo diet started may not be necessary information to you, but it can explain the science behind it and why it became so popular, for all the skeptics out there.

Surprisingly, and arguably, the idea of a diet revolving around our Paleolithic ancestors was inspired by the works of Charles Darwin and his theorizing of how evolution works. Evolutionarily speaking, we humans (both as cavemen and as their modern counterparts) are designed to live a certain way to maintain peak health. Think about it – when we first discovered fire, do you think we would have survived long if all we ate was fast food? Probably not.

Rather, as evolution suggests, the fittest will survive in the long run. While this doesn't mean whoever is physically fit will survive (the notion of "fitness" has more to do with adaptability in the context of evolutionary science), our ancestors would not have fared well if they were as overweight as many individuals are today.

Lucky for us, we don't need to constantly chase our food (or run from the threat of being something else's food) thanks to advancements in technology and science. We lead pretty cushy lives, and because of that we don't need to stay in top physical shape to avoid being eaten or killed.

So, diets were created and tested in order to maintain a healthy lifestyle alongside an increasingly sedentary way of life. Some worked alright, others didn't provide any results. In the mid-1980s, however, more and more nutritionists started writing about the ways our cavemen ancestors found and ate food, and how their diets differed from our own. Those nutritionists noticed a lack of several types of food (which we consider staple food today) and put it to reason that our lack of overall healthiness derives less from a lack of exercise (although it doesn't help) and more from an increase in certain foods we ingest.

Many people came to the conclusion that stable farming has a lot to do with the change in humanity's collective biological differences between us and our ancestors. With farming comes one type of food that plays a large role in how our body interacts with foods and how we utilize the energy we ingest: carbohydrates. Before farming, humans had no way of storing and eating large quantities of carb-heavy foods. This change is one of the most major differences between humanity then and humanity now. We'll talk more about carbohydrates in a later section.

Anyhow, skip ahead to 2007. For several decades, people have gone on TV and tried to sell easy cures to obesity and one-step weight loss programs. People were desperate for a diet or lifestyle to help them stay in shape. Quickly, and seemingly out of nowhere, people begin to talk about these papers from nearly twenty years prior – papers about the Paleolithic diet and the differences between our diet and the diets of our ancestors. Groups of individuals put the theory to the test and started to rely on more natural foods (like those of our ancestors) and noticed drastic changes to their body weight, their energy levels, and their overall health. These changes came as a shock because, despite the drastic increase in health, those individuals didn't need to put in a lot of the effort as they did with the other diets they had tried. In fact, it almost came naturally to many of them.

Finally, skip ahead to 2014. The Paleo diet has spiked in popularity and people can't get enough. Large sample sizes of hundreds of thousands of people have shown that the diet offers generally positive results with relatively minimal effort. Those who thought the diet was another hipster fad are seeing the benefits on a large scale, scientists are looking into the chemical changes in the body that come about due to the diet, and people are beginning to take the diet seriously.

Like tons of different things in the world, the Paleo diet started out as a small niche of people trying something new. This small group who tested the Paleo diet noticed results and went on to tell others about it. Papers were published, scientific studies were performed, and people all over the world began to see the benefits of the diet.

Chapter 3: Proper Foods to Eat

The Paleo diet does have a fairly strict list of foods you can and cannot eat, but the list of foods that you *are* able to eat contains so many foods that you may not even realize there are rules in place. The Paleo diet, while avoiding foods most people are willing to declare unhealthy (frozen and preservative-filled foods), also works more to educate you on how much unnecessary processing goes into everyday foods and how you can avoid ingesting too many processed ingredients.

Meats are a great way to get protein and fats for energy without having to rely on sugars or carbs (we'll get into how bad carbs can sometimes be in the next section). When many people think "meat," they may easily first jump to the image of frozen chicken nuggets in a bag. These are not good! These are processed and should be avoided.

What the general Paleo diet doctrine suggests is high-quality hormone-free meats, just like the meats you (or your cavemen ancestors) would find out in the wild grazing naturally. These meats are not bulked up with steroids and live a relatively healthy life before being eaten. Buying raw meat (whether you buy it from the butcher or buy it straight from the farm) allows you to monitor every step of its preparation and cooking so that you know there are no preservatives or other mysterious steps involved.

Back in the old days, our ancestors could find a huge variety of meats, such as red meats from cows, white meats from turkeys and chickens, and fish from rivers. Just like the cavemen, you are not limited to eating only one kind of meat, and you shouldn't completely avoid red meat by any means. Rather, focus on the quality of the meat and where the meat comes from.

As our ancestors were also gatherers, fruits and vegetables were a huge part of their diets as well. Fruits and berries would be picked fresh from the vine and eaten as they were. If you go apple picking in the fall, you are participating in the exact same steps to collecting your food. Fruits should be typically eaten raw for their full benefits, but that doesn't mean don't be creative.

Vegetables are much more versatile and many require cooking or steaming before they can be fully enjoyed. Like meats, there are a lot of farms out there that rely on chemicals and steroids to produce the "best" veggies they can. While these may not be the worst things to put into your body, organic vegetables should always be your first choice when shopping.

Better yet, one way you know our ancestors would have eaten something is if you can grow it yourself. Anything you can grow in your backyard (aside from grains) will make a perfect addition to the Paleo diet. While our ancestors didn't have farming, growing fruits and vegetables is the closest you will come to finding a stalk of broccoli in the wild if you live in the suburbs.

Foods that you should definitely eat while on the Paleo diet:

1. Fruits
2. Oils and fats
3. Vegetables (cooked or raw, it's up to you!)
4. Meats (as additive- and chemical-free as you can find)
5. Nuts and seeds
6. Seafood

Chapter 4: Foods to Avoid

Back in the days of hunting and gathering, our ancestors relied on only the foods that they could, well, hunt and gather. Humans had not discovered the ease of farming yet, so all of their food was seasonal and in small number. Because there was no farming to take advantage of, our ancestors lacked one food that people tend to overeat in the modern world: grains.

That's right, no oats, no pasta, no quinoa, and no cereal. Whereas meats contain mostly proteins and (healthy) fats, and fruits contain natural sugars and a whole slew of vitamins, grains consist mostly of things called carbohydrates, which do not interact well with our body.

While those proteins and fats from meat products build our muscles and give us fast-burning energy respectively, and the vitamins from fruit help to balance the chemicals in our bodies, the carbohydrates in grains become slower-burning sugars when we ingest them. While this sounds like it could be helpful for long-term activities, and some will argue that it definitely is, those slow-burning sugars are converted to fat if not used, which is then stored in the body for when it needs to burn off a little excess energy. If you weren't going to eat for a day or two after eating a large bowl of spaghetti, that extra fat may be alright, but if you plan on enjoying a meal or two the following day, you would just be placing more energy to burn over the fat, so that extra fat (and the extra inch around your waist) won't be burned off, and will in fact stick around for a while.

In short, avoid grains while following the Paleo diet.

One food group that many Paleo dieters tend to be on the fence about is dairy. While milk is technically found in nature, it's a bit odd that humans drink other animals' milk, isn't it? Milk is created within animal bodies in order to provide sustenance for that creature's young, whether we're talking about humans, cats, or *any* mammal.

Typically, in the animal kingdom, older siblings and adults are lactose intolerant to milk from any source. This evolutionary trait allows younger siblings, who can't go out and find food on their own, to drink their mother's milk. Humans have forcibly ignored this natural progression and forced ourselves to continue to drink milk after we've long stopped needed our own mother's milk.

Humans are weird for this, but it's normal within society. In short, drinking milk (from any animal) is up to you as an individual, but it should never be a common drink of choice because of how dense it is in calories.

Processed foods are foods that every dietician and high school health teacher will tell you to avoid – and for good reason! Processed foods tend to be high in fat and sugars. All the negatives aside, you know for a fact that our ancestors couldn't have gone to the closest grocery store and picked up a bag of processed burritos.

Processed foods are tricky because they are everywhere in the world today. Ninety-nine percent of the foods in the freezer section are processed to some degree. All snack foods, chips, pre-packaged cookies, and fast food are also almost entirely made out of processed foods with high levels of corn syrup. It's hard to avoid processed foods in the modern world, but that's all the more reason to do so.

Our cavemen ancestors didn't have the methods to produce processed foods and high concentrations of corn syrup, so avoid those at all costs!

One easy way to track what may be processed (and therefore less natural, and *therefore* less healthy) is to check the shelf life. Typically, the longer the shelf life, the more processing the food underwent or the more preservatives in the food itself (preservatives should also be avoided), which means it's a food that our ancestors wouldn't have had access to.

Of course, there are exceptions. Some foods have naturally longer shelf lives than others (honey, for example, doesn't go bad despite being all natural). It's best to research foods before grabbing them in bulk anyways.

For those who just want to see a quick list, here's a quick list of foods you should avoid:

1. Legumes (including peanuts)
2. All types of grains (including cereals, rice, wheat and bread)
3. White potatoes
4. Dairy products
5. Highly-processed foods
6. Refined sugars (which is also found in corn syrup)

Chapter 5: Parting Remarks

Now you know some of the basics of the Paleo diet and the foods that our ancestors ate to stay as healthy as they were. It's now up to you to decide if you want to move forward with this exciting new lifestyle, or try another option. This diet may not be for every single person out there, but remember all diets take work and self-discipline, so be prepared to struggle through temptation and be healthier for it.

Let's now get into the recipes!

Enjoy!

Breakfast
Eggplant and Olive Spread

Prep Time: 5 minutes; **Cook Time:** 3 minutes

Pressure Level: High; **Release Type:** Natural

Serving Size: 270g; **Serves:** 4; **Calories:** 216

Total Fat: 17.5g **Saturated Fat:** 2.4g; **Trans Fat:** 0g

Protein: 3.1g; **Net Carbs:** 6.6g

Total Carbs: 15g; **Dietary Fiber:** 8.4g; **Sugars:** 7g

Cholesterol: 0mg; **Sodium:** 454mg; **Potassium:** 554mg;

Vitamin A: 0%; **Vitamin C:** 18%; **Calcium:** 4%; **Iron:** 5%.

Ingredients:
- 4 tablespoons olive oil
- 2 pounds eggplant
- 3 cloves garlic, skin on
- 1 teaspoon salt
- 1 cup water
- juice of 1 lemon
- 1 tablespoon tahini
- ¼ cup black olives, pitted

Directions:
1. Slice the eggplant into a few large chunks to cover the bottom of the pressure cooker with them. Chop the rest of them into smaller pieces.
2. Set the pressure cooker to "Sauté" and heat the olive oil. Place the larger chunks of eggplant in and fry them for about 5 minutes. Add the whole garlic cloves.
3. Flip the eggplant over and toss in the remaining eggplant pieces, salt and water.
4. Seal the lid and cook for 3 minutes at high pressure.
5. When done, release the pressure naturally.
6. Discard the liquid. Remove the garlic and peel off the skin.

7. Place the tahini, lemon juice, garlic cloves, olives and cooked eggplant into a blender and puree until smooth.

Carrot Cashew Smoothie

Prep Time: 10 minutes; **Cook Time:** 4 minutes

Pressure Level: High; **Release Type:** Natural

Serving Size: 86g; **Serves:** 4; **Calories:** 161

Total Fat: 9.5g **Saturated Fat:** 1.8g; **Trans Fat:** 0g

Protein: 4g; **Net Carbs:** 13.8g

Total Carbs: 15.8g; **Dietary Fiber:** 2g; **Sugars:** 8.3g

Cholesterol: 0mg; **Sodium:** 45mg; **Potassium:** 198mg;

Vitamin A: 204%; **Vitamin C:** 6%; **Calcium:** 3%; **Iron:** 11%.

Ingredients:
- ☐ 2 cups fresh carrots, chopped
- ☐ ½ cup cashews
- ☐ 2 teaspoons honey

Directions:
1. Add the carrots and cashews into the pressure cooker and cover with 2 cups of water. Cook for 4 minutes at high pressure. Let the pressure release naturally when done.
2. Transfer everything, including the carrot broth, into a blender. Add honey and blend until perfectly smooth.
3. Let it chill completely before serving.

Korean Style Steamed Eggs

Prep Time: 10 minutes; **Cook Time:** 5 minutes

Pressure Level: High; **Release Type:** Quick

Serving Size: 52g; **Serves:** 3; **Calories:** 84

Total Fat: 5.6g **Saturated Fat:** 1.7g; **Trans Fat:** 0g

Protein: 6.7g; **Net Carbs:** 1.1g

Total Carbs: 1.4g; **Dietary Fiber:** 0.3g; **Sugars:** 0.8g

Cholesterol: 186mg; **Sodium:** 71mg; **Potassium:** 86mg;

Vitamin A: 5%; **Vitamin C:** 0%; **Calcium:** 4%; **Iron:** 6%.

Ingredients:
- ☐ 3 large eggs
- ☐ 1 cup water
- ☐ chopped scallions, to taste
- ☐ 1 teaspoon sesame seeds
- ☐ 1 teaspoon garlic powder
- ☐ sea salt and pepper, to taste

Directions:
1. In a small bowl, whisk together the eggs and water.
2. Put the egg mixture into a heat proof bowl, toss in the remaining ingredients and stir well.
3. Pour 1 to 2 cups of water into the inner pot of the pressure cooker. Set the trivet in its place.
4. Place the heat proof bowl onto the trivet.
5. Seal the lid and set the timer to 5 minutes at high pressure.
6. When done, release the pressure quickly.
7. Serve right away.

Breakfast Quiche

Prep Time: 10 minutes; **Cook Time:** 30 minutes

Pressure Level: High; **Release Type:** Quick

Serving Size: 160g; **Serves:** 4; **Calories:** 243

Total Fat: 17.5g **Saturated Fat:** 6.3g; **Trans Fat:** 0g

Protein: 18.3g; **Net Carbs:** 1.9g

Total Carbs: 2.4g; **Dietary Fiber:** 0.5g; **Sugars:** 1.7g

Cholesterol: 306mg; **Sodium:** 735mg; **Potassium:** 185mg;

Vitamin A: 13%; **Vitamin C:** 10%; **Calcium:** 11%; **Iron:** 12%.

Ingredients:
- ☐ 6 large eggs, well beaten
- ☐ ½ cup almond milk
- ☐ ¼ teaspoon sea salt
- ☐ 4 slices bacon, cooked and crumbled
- ☐ 1 cup cooked ground sausage
- ☐ ½ cup diced ham
- ☐ 2 large green onions, chopped

Directions:
1. Set the trivet in its place and pour 1 to 2 cups of water into the inner pot of the pressure cooker.
2. Whisk together the eggs, almond milk and salt in a large bowl.
3. Place the bacon, sausage, diced ham and green onions into a 1-quart soufflé dish. Stir well, then pour the egg mixture over the meat. Stir to combine.
4. Cover the dish with aluminum foil.
5. Seal the lid and set the timer to 30 minutes at high pressure.
6. When done, release the pressure quickly.
7. Open the lid, remove the dish and uncover the foil.
8. Serve right away.

Egg Muffins

Prep Time: 10 minutes; **Cook Time:** 8 minutes

Pressure Level: High; **Release Type:** Quick

Serving Size: 94g; **Serves:** 4; **Calories:** 113

Total Fat: 6.6g **Saturated Fat:** 2.4g; **Trans Fat:** 0g

Protein: 9.7g; **Net Carbs:** 2.4g

Total Carbs: 2.9g; **Dietary Fiber:** 0.5g; **Sugars:** 2.2g

Cholesterol: 193mg; **Sodium**: 177mg; **Potassium**: 135mg;

Vitamin A: 26%; **Vitamin C**: 104%; **Calcium**: 3%; **Iron**: 6%.

Ingredients:

☐   4 eggs
☐   ¼ teaspoon lemon pepper seasoning
☐   1 green onion, diced
☐   1 cup diced red bell pepper
☐   4 slices precooked bacon, crumbled

Directions:

1.   Place the steamer basket into the pressure cooker and pour 1 to 2 cups of water into the inner pot.
2.   Whisk together the eggs and lemon pepper.
3.   Evenly distribute the onion, red bell pepper and bacon among four silicone muffin cups. Pour the egg mixture into each muffin cup and stir to combine.
4.   Place the cups onto the steamer basket. Seal the lid and set the timer to 8 minutes at high pressure.
5.   When done, release the pressure quickly.
6.   Serve right away or store in the fridge for up to a week. Reheat in the microwave when needed.

French Baked Eggs

Prep Time: 5 minutes; **Cook Time:** 4 minutes

Pressure Level: Low; **Release Type:** Natural

Serving Size: 60g; **Serves:** 4; **Calories:** 132

Total Fat: 10g **Saturated Fat:** 2.8g; **Trans Fat:** 0g

Protein: 9.3g; **Net Carbs:** 0g

Total Carbs: 0.4g; **Dietary Fiber:** 0.4g; **Sugars:** 0.6g

Cholesterol: 193mg; **Sodium:** 176mg; **Potassium:** 69mg;

Vitamin A: 5%; **Vitamin C:** 7%; **Calcium:** 3%; **Iron:** 5%.

Ingredients:
- 4 eggs
- 4 slices of bacon
- 4 slices of vegetable of choice
- 4 garnish of fresh herbs
- olive oil, to taste

Directions:
1. Place the trivet into the pressure cooker and pour 1 to 2 cups of water into the inner pot.
2. Add a drop of olive oil into each of the four ramekins and rub the bottom.
3. Lay a slice of bacon and a vegetable into each of them. Then break an egg on top of each vegetable. Sprinkle with fresh herbs and a few drops of oil.
4. Place the ramekins onto the trivet and put it in the pressure cooker.
5. Seal the lid and set the timer to 4 minutes at low pressure.
6. When done, release the pressure naturally.
7. Serve right away.

Lunch
Chicken Red Cabbage Soup

Prep Time: 15 minutes; **Cook Time:** 30 minutes

Pressure Level: High; **Release Type:** Natural

Serving Size: 380g; **Serves**: 6; **Calories:** 478

Total Fat: 28.4g **Saturated Fat:** 10.1g; **Trans Fat:** 0g

Protein: 44.1g; **Net Carbs:** 42.1g

Total Carbs: 13.1g; **Dietary Fiber:** 3g; **Sugars:** 8g

Cholesterol: 161mg; **Sodium:** 194mg; **Potassium:** 297mg;

Vitamin A: 84%; **Vitamin C**: 96%; **Calcium**: 4%; **Iron**: 16%.

Ingredients:
- ☐ 1 medium (3-pound) chicken, cleaned
- ☐ 1 red onion, sliced
- ☐ 2 cloves garlic, smashed
- ☐ ½ medium red cabbage, thinly slices
- ☐ 2 large carrots, sliced
- ☐ water, enough to cover
- ☐ 1 teaspoon ginger powder
- ☐ 1 teaspoon turmeric powder
- ☐ 1 teaspoon cinnamon powder
- ☐ 1 lime
- ☐ ½ pineapple, cut into small chunks
- ☐ 2 spring onions, finely sliced

Directions:
1. Place the chicken, onion, garlic, red cabbage and carrots into the pressure cooker. Pour in enough water to cover everything.
2. Seal the lid and set the pressure cooker to "Soup" function for 25 to 30 minutes.
3. When done, release the pressure naturally.
4. Remove the chicken and shred it to bite-size pieces. Then return the meat back into the pressure cooker.

5. Add the spices, pineapple and the juice of half of the lime. Set the pressure cooker to "Sauté" and let it cook for another 10 minutes.
6. Serve with sliced spring onions and a few slices of lime.

Chinese Pork Ribs

Prep Time: 30 minutes; **Cook Time:** 15 minutes

Pressure Level: High; **Release Type:** Natural

Serving Size: 162g; **Serves:** 8; **Calories:** 365

Total Fat: 26.7g **Saturated Fat:** 10.3g; **Trans Fat:** 0g

Protein: 24g; **Net Carbs:** 7.7g

Total Carbs: 8.1g; **Dietary Fiber:** 0.4g; **Sugars:** 1.1g

Cholesterol: 68mg; **Sodium:** 771mg; **Potassium:** 29mg;

Vitamin A: 1%; **Vitamin C:** 4%; **Calcium:** 1%; **Iron:** 6%.

Ingredients:
- 2.5 pounds pork spareribs, diced
- 1 teaspoon maple syrup
- 1 tablespoon sesame oil
- 1 tablespoon coconut aminos
- 1 tablespoon dry sherry
- 1 teaspoon sea salt
- 1 teaspoon ground black pepper
- ¼ cup garlic cloves, sliced
- 1 tablespoon ginger, grated
- ½ cup minced green onions
- 2 teaspoons almond flour
- 1 cup water

Directions:
1. In a large mixing bowl, combine the maple syrup, sesame oil, aminos, sherry, salt and pepper, beans, garlic, ginger and green onions.
2. Toss in the diced spareribs and stir well. Let it marinate at room temperature for 30 minutes.
3. In a small bowl, combine the almond flour and water. Pour into the bowl with the spareribs.
4. Transfer everything to the pressure cooker and seal the lid. Cook for 15 minutes at high pressure.
5. When done, release the pressure naturally.

Italian Wedding Soup

Prep Time: 15 minutes; **Cook Time:** 10 minutes

Pressure Level: High; **Release Type:** Quick

Serving Size: 681g; **Serves:** 4; **Calories:** 380

Total Fat: 17.5g **Saturated Fat:** 6.2g; **Trans Fat:** 0g

Protein: 33.6g; **Net Carbs:** 15.2g

Total Carbs: 18.1g; **Dietary Fiber:** 2.9g; **Sugars:** 8.7g

Cholesterol: 80mg; **Sodium:** 1743mg; **Potassium:** 702mg;

Vitamin A: 118%; **Vitamin C:** 10%; **Calcium:** 9%; **Iron:** 17%.

Ingredients:
Meatballs
- ☐ 1 pound ground turkey
- ☐ 3 tablespoons almond flour
- ☐ 3 tablespoons coconut milk
- ☐ 1 tablespoon maple syrup
- ☐ 1 teaspoon garlic powder
- ☐ pinch sea salt

Soup
- ☐ 1 tablespoon avocado oil
- ☐ 1 medium onion, diced
- ☐ 7 ½ cups chicken broth
- ☐ 1 cup carrots, diced
- ☐ ½ teaspoon onion powder
- ☐ ½ teaspoon garlic powder
- ☐ ½ teaspoon sea salt
- ☐ 1 cup spinach, chopped

Directions:
1. Preheat the oven to 350 degrees F.
2. Combine all the meatball ingredients and mix them well by hand. Form 2-inch meatballs and place them on a baking sheet lined with parchment paper.
3. Bake for about 10 to 12 minutes and remove the pan from the oven.

4. Set the pressure cooker to "Sauté", heat 1 tablespoon of avocado oil and toss in the onion. Sauté until the onion turns translucent.
5. Add in the chicken broth, baked meatballs, carrots, onion powder, garlic powder and salt.
6. Seal the lid and cook for 10 minutes at high pressure.
7. When done, release the pressure quickly.
8. Open the lid and toss in the spinach. Stir until the spinach is wilted.
9. Ladle into individual bowls and serve warm.

Shredded Salsa Chicken

Prep Time: 5 minutes; **Cook Time:** 15 minutes

Pressure Level: High; **Release Type:** Quick

Serving Size: 210g; **Serves:** 4; **Calories:** 167

Total Fat: 4.2g **Saturated Fat:** 1.5g; **Trans Fat:** 0g

Protein: 26.6g; **Net Carbs:** 4.5g

Total Carbs: 6.1g; **Dietary Fiber:** 1.6g; **Sugars:** 3g

Cholesterol: 65mg; **Sodium:** 820mg; **Potassium:** 290mg;

Vitamin A: 6%; **Vitamin C:** 3%; **Calcium:** 3%; **Iron:** 7%.

Ingredients:
- ☐ 1 pound chicken breasts
- ☐ 1 ½ cups homemade tomato salsa
- ☐ ½ teaspoon sea salt
- ☐ ¼ teaspoon black pepper
- ☐ ½ teaspoon garlic powder

Directions:
1. Place all the ingredients in the pressure cooker and stir well.
2. Seal the lid and press the "Poultry" button. This will let it cook for 15 minutes at high pressure.
3. When done, use the quick release method and open the lid.
4. Serve immediately.

Pina Colada Chicken

Prep Time: 10 minutes; **Cook Time:** 15 minutes

Pressure Level: High; **Release Type:** Natural

Serving Size: 309g; **Serves**: 4; **Calories:** 505

Total Fat: 28.3g **Saturated Fat:** 16.3g; **Trans Fat**: 0g

Protein: 45.8g; **Net Carbs:** 11.6g

Total Carbs: 13g; **Dietary Fiber:** 1.4g; **Sugars:** 4.6g

Cholesterol: 190mg; **Sodium**: 232mg; **Potassium**: 60mg;

Vitamin A: 1%; **Vitamin C**: 48%; **Calcium**: 1%; **Iron**: 12%.

Ingredients:
- ☐ 2 pounds chicken thighs, cut into 1-inch chunks
- ☐ 1 cup fresh pineapple chunks
- ☐ ½ cup full-fat coconut cream
- ☐ 1 teaspoon cinnamon
- ☐ 1 pinch sea salt
- ☐ ½ cup chopped green onion

Directions:
1. Place the chicken thighs, pineapple, coconut cream, cinnamon and salt in the pressure cooker.
2. Seal the lid and press the "Poultry" button. This will let it cook for 15 minutes at high pressure.
3. When done, release the pressure naturally.
4. Sprinkle with chopped green onion before serving.

Cabbage Soup

Prep Time: 10 minutes; **Cook Time:** 5 minutes

Pressure Level: High; **Release Type:** Natural

Serving Size: 807g; **Serves:** 4; **Calories:** 419

Total Fat: 17.5g **Saturated Fat:** 6.8g; **Trans Fat:** 0g

Protein: 39g; **Net Carbs:** 19.7g

Total Carbs: 28.6g; **Dietary Fiber:** 8.9g; **Sugars:** 10.3g

Cholesterol: 78mg; **Sodium:** 824mg; **Potassium:** 874mg;

Vitamin A: 127%; **Vitamin C:** 162%; **Calcium:** 14%; **Iron:** 13%.

Ingredients:
- ☐ 1 teaspoon ghee
- ☐ 1 small onion, diced
- ☐ sea salt, to taste
- ☐ 1 pound ground pork
- ☐ 6 large fresh shiitake mushrooms, stemmed and thinly sliced
- ☐ 2 garlic cloves, minced
- ☐ 6 cups bone broth
- ☐ 2 pounds cabbage, chopped
- ☐ 2 large carrots, peeled and sliced into coins
- ☐ 1 large sweet potato, peeled and cubed
- ☐ 3 scallions, thinly sliced

Directions:
1. Set the pressure cooker to "Sauté", melt the ghee and toss in the diced onion and salt.
2. Sauté the onions for about 3 minutes.
3. Toss in the ground pork and stir well with a spatula. Then, stir in the sliced mushrooms as well. Cook for about 5 to 7 minutes.
4. Stir in the garlic and cook for another 30 seconds.
5. Pour in the broth and bring to a boil. Stir in the chopped cabbage, carrots, cubed potato and sliced scallions.

6. Seal the lid and cook for 5 minutes at high pressure.
7. When done, release the pressure naturally.
8. Ladle into individual bowls and serve warm.

Broccoli Soup

Prep Time: 15 minutes; **Cook Time:** 5 minutes

Pressure Level: High; **Release Type:** Natural

Serving Size: 391g; **Serves:** 6; **Calories:** 123

Total Fat: 5.9g **Saturated Fat:** 4.7g; **Trans Fat:** 0g

Protein: 6.4g; **Net Carbs:** 10.5g

Total Carbs: 14.3g; **Dietary Fiber:** 3.8g; **Sugars:** 4.3g

Cholesterol: 0mg; **Sodium:** 514mg; **Potassium:** 432mg;

Vitamin A: 17%; **Vitamin C:** 172%; **Calcium:** 9%; **Iron:** 9%.

Ingredients:
- 2 tablespoons coconut oil
- 3 medium leeks, white parts only, roughly chopped
- 2 medium shallots, roughly chopped
- ½ teaspoon sea salt
- 1 ½ pounds broccoli, chopped into florets
- ¼ cup apple, peeled and diced
- 4 cups chicken stock
- 1 cup coconut milk

Directions:
1. Set the pressure cooker to "Sauté", heat the coconut oil and toss in the chopped leeks, shallots and salt.
2. Cook, while stirring frequently, for about 5 minutes.
3. Stir in the chopped broccoli and diced apple.
4. Pour in the chicken stock and make sure all the vegetables are covered with liquid. If not, add some more water.
5. Press the "Cancel/Keep Warm" button on the pressure cooker and position it under the stovetop vent.
6. Seal the lid and cook for 5 minutes at high pressure.
7. When cooked, release the pressure naturally under the stovetop vent.
8. Transfer the content into a blender and blend until smooth. Pour in the coconut milk and blend some more.

9. Serve immediately.

Creamy Onion Soup

Prep Time: 20 minutes; **Cook Time:** 10 minutes

Pressure Level: High; **Release Type:** Natural

Serving Size: 692g; **Serves:** 4; **Calories:** 213

Total Fat: 7.3g **Saturated Fat:** 6g; **Trans Fat:** 0g

Protein: 8g; **Net Carbs:** 25g

Total Carbs: 31.9g; **Dietary Fiber:** 6.9g; **Sugars:** 14.1g

Cholesterol: 0mg; **Sodium:** 1318mg; **Potassium:** 467mg;

Vitamin A: 0%; **Vitamin C:** 37%; **Calcium:** 7%; **Iron:** 4%.

Ingredients:
- ☐ 2 tablespoons coconut oil
- ☐ 8 cups yellow onions, sliced
- ☐ 1 tablespoon balsamic vinegar
- ☐ 6 cups pork stock
- ☐ 1 teaspoon sea salt
- ☐ 2 bay leaves
- ☐ 2 sprigs fresh thyme

Directions:
1. Set the pressure cooker to "Sauté", heat the olive oil and toss in the onions. Sauté for about 15 minutes, stirring occasionally.
2. Pour in the balsamic vinegar and pork stock. Add the salt, bay leaves and fresh thyme.
3. Seal the lid and set the timer to 10 minutes at high pressure.
4. When done, release the pressure naturally.
5. Remove the bay leaves and thyme stems. Transfer the soup into a blender and blend until smooth.
6. Serve warm.

Cherry Tomato Chicken Cacciatore

Prep Time: 15 minutes; **Cook Time:** 14 minutes	

Prep Time: 15 minutes; **Cook Time:** 14 minutes

Pressure Level: High; **Release Type:** Natural

Serving Size: 488g; **Serves**: 4; **Calories:** 475

Total Fat: 15.5g **Saturated Fat:** 0.3g; **Trans Fat:** 0g

Protein: 66.1g; **Net Carbs:** 4.6g

Total Carbs: 5.6g; **Dietary Fiber:** 1g; **Sugars:** 2.9g

Cholesterol: 285mg; **Sodium**: 925mg; **Potassium**: 25mg;

Vitamin A: 11%; **Vitamin C**: 60%; **Calcium**: 2%; **Iron**: 21%.

Ingredients:
- ☐ 1 teaspoon olive oil
- ☐ 3 pounds bone-in chicken legs and thighs
- ☐ 1 pound cherry tomatoes
- ☐ 2 garlic cloves, minced
- ☐ 1 teaspoon sea salt
- ☐ ¼ cup red table wine
- ☐ 1 cup water
- ☐ 1 sprig fresh basil leaves, torn
- ☐ ½ cup pitted green olives, sliced

Directions:
1. Set the pressure cooker to "Sauté", heat the olive oil and brown the chicken thighs.
2. Meanwhile, place the cherry tomatoes in a large Ziploc bag, close the bag, but leave a tiny hole at the end. Using a meat pounder, lightly crush all of the cherry tomatoes to burst them open.
3. Pour the cherry tomato mixture into the pressure cooker. Add the minced garlic, salt, wine and water and stir well.
4. Seal the lid and cook for 14 minutes at high pressure. When done, release the pressure naturally.
5. Ladle the soup into individual bowls and sprinkle with basil leaves and green olives before serving.

Chicken Taco Filling

Prep Time: 20 minutes; **Cook Time:** 15 minutes

Pressure Level: High; **Release Type:** Quick

Serving Size: 263g; **Serves:** 4; **Calories:** 231

Total Fat: 7.3g **Saturated Fat:** 0.5g; **Trans Fat:** 0g

Protein: 32.9g; **Net Carbs:** 5.1g

Total Carbs: 7.1g; **Dietary Fiber:** 2g; **Sugars:** 4g

Cholesterol: 96mg; **Sodium:** 619mg; **Potassium:** 610mg;

Vitamin A: 7%; **Vitamin C:** 17%; **Calcium:** 3%; **Iron:** 4%.

Ingredients:
- ☐ 1 tablespoon olive oil
- ☐ 1 large onion, diced
- ☐ 6 large chicken breasts
- ☐ 1 (10-ounce) can diced tomatoes
- ☐ 1 tablespoon chili powder
- ☐ 1 teaspoon sea salt

Directions:
1. Set the pressure cooker to "Sauté", heat the olive oil and toss in the chopped onion. Sauté the onion until tender, for about 10 minutes.
2. Toss in the chicken breasts, diced tomatoes, chili powder and salt.
3. Seal the lid and cook for 15 minutes at high pressure. When done, use the quick release method.
4. Remove the chicken from the pressure cooker, shred it and place it back into it. Stir all the ingredients well.
5. Set the pressure cooker to "Sauté" and cook uncovered until all the liquid is absorbed.
6. Serve immediately.

Kale with Garlic

Prep Time: 10 minutes; **Cook Time:** 5 minutes

Pressure Level: High; **Release Type:** Quick

Serving Size: 125g; **Serves:** 4; **Calories:** 90

Total Fat: 3.6g **Saturated Fat:** 0.5g; **Trans Fat:** 0g

Protein: 3.5g; **Net Carbs:** 10.8g

Total Carbs: 12.6g; **Dietary Fiber:** 1.8g; **Sugars:** 0.1g

Cholesterol: 0mg; **Sodium:** 245mg; **Potassium:** 569mg;

Vitamin A: 346%; **Vitamin C:** 231%; **Calcium:** 16%; **Iron:** 11%.

Ingredients:
- ☐ 1 tablespoon olive oil
- ☐ 3 cloves garlic, slivered
- ☐ 1 pound kale, cleaned and stems trimmed
- ☐ ½ cup water
- ☐ ½ teaspoon sea salt
- ☐ juice from ½ lemon

Directions:
1. Set the pressure cooker to "Sauté", heat the olive oil and toss in the garlic. Sauté for a minute, then add in the kale. Season with salt and pour in the water.
2. Seal the lid and cook for 5 minutes at high pressure. When done, quick release the pressure, then remove the lid.
3. Drizzle with the juice from ½ of the lemon and serve.

Asparagus Soup

Prep Time: 10 minutes; **Cook Time:** 45 minutes

Pressure Level: High; **Release Type:** Natural

Serving Size: 603g; **Serves:** 4; **Calories:** 238

Total Fat: 14.4g **Saturated Fat:** 8g; **Trans Fat:** 0g

Protein: 15.4g; **Net Carbs:** 9.4g

Total Carbs: 14.5g; **Dietary Fiber:** 5.1g; **Sugars:** 7g

Cholesterol: 41mg; **Sodium:** 1258mg; **Potassium:** 676mg;

Vitamin A: 34%; **Vitamin C:** 26%; **Calcium:** 8%; **Iron:** 34%.

Ingredients:
- ☐ 3 tablespoons ghee
- ☐ 1 white onion, diced
- ☐ 5 cloves garlic, pressed
- ☐ 1 cup diced ham
- ☐ 4 cups chicken broth
- ☐ 2 pounds asparagus, split
- ☐ salt and pepper, to taste

Directions:
1. Set the pressure cooker to "Sauté" and heat the ghee.
2. Toss in the onion and sauté for about 5 minutes.
3. Add the garlic, ham and chicken broth. Let it simmer for about 3 minutes.
4. Lastly, add the asparagus and seal the lid.
5. Cook for 45 minutes on "Soup" setting.
6. When done, release the pressure naturally.

Egg Roll Soup

Prep Time: 15 minutes; **Cook Time:** 25 minutes

Pressure Level: High; **Release Type:** Quick

Serving Size: 416g; **Serves:** 6; **Calories:** 214

Total Fat: 9.4g **Saturated Fat:** 4.3g; **Trans Fat:** 0g

Protein: 18.5g; **Net Carbs:** 11.1g

Total Carbs: 14.7g; **Dietary Fiber:** 3.6g; **Sugars:** 6.2g

Cholesterol: 62mg; **Sodium:** 1128mg; **Potassium:** 468mg;

Vitamin A: 139%; **Vitamin C:** 74%; **Calcium:** 8%; **Iron:** 3%.

Ingredients:
- ☐ 1 tablespoon ghee
- ☐ 1 pound ground pastured pork
- ☐ 1 large onion, diced
- ☐ 4 cups beef broth
- ☐ ½ head cabbage, chopped
- ☐ 2 cups shredded carrots
- ☐ 1 teaspoon garlic powder
- ☐ 1 teaspoon onion powder
- ☐ 1 teaspoon sea salt
- ☐ 1 teaspoon ground ginger
- ☐ 2/3 cup coconut aminos

Directions:
1. Set the pressure cooker to "Sauté", heat the ghee and toss in the diced onion and pork. Cook until the meat is no longer pink.
2. Toss in all the remaining ingredients.
3. Seal the lid and set the timer to 25 minutes at high pressure.
4. When done, release the pressure quickly.
5. Open the lid and serve right away.

Cabbage Apple Stew

Prep Time: 5 minutes; **Cook Time:** 20 minutes

Pressure Level: High; **Release Type:** Natural

Serving Size: 504g; **Serves:** 4; **Calories:** 123

Total Fat: 0.1g **Saturated Fat:** 0g; **Trans Fat:** 0g

Protein: 13.1g; **Net Carbs:** 14.3g

Total Carbs: 19.8g; **Dietary Fiber:** 5.5g; **Sugars:** 11.8g

Cholesterol: 0mg; **Sodium:** 527mg; **Potassium:** 511mg;

Vitamin A: 86%; **Vitamin C:** 118%; **Calcium:** 9%; **Iron:** 18%.

Ingredients:
- 4 cups bone broth
- 1 apple, peeled and diced
- 1 head cabbage, chopped
- 1 small onion, chopped
- 2 small carrots, chopped
- 1 tablespoon fresh ginger, grated
- 1 teaspoon gelatin
- 2 tablespoons parsley
- sea salt, to taste

Directions:
1. Place all of the ingredients into the pressure cooker.
2. Set the timer to 20 minutes at high pressure.
3. When done, release the pressure naturally.
4. Serve warm.

Chipotle Carnitas Bowl

Prep Time: 30 minutes; **Cook Time:** 42 minutes

Pressure Level: High; **Release Type:** Natural

Serving Size: 292g; **Serves**: 8; **Calories:** 557

Total Fat: 43.2g **Saturated Fat:** 18.6g; **Trans Fat**: 0g

Protein: 39.4g; **Net Carbs:** 1.6g

Total Carbs: 1.7g; **Dietary Fiber:** 0.1g; **Sugars:** 0.4g

Cholesterol: 161mg; **Sodium:** 669mg; **Potassium**: 13mg;

Vitamin A: 3%; **Vitamin C:** 5%; **Calcium:** 0%; **Iron**: 17%.

Ingredients:
- ☐ 4 pounds pork shoulder butt
- ☐ 4 tablespoons ghee
- ☐ 6 cloves garlic, finely chopped
- ☐ 2 teaspoons sea salt
- ☐ 1 teaspoon black pepper
- ☐ 1 teaspoon garlic powder
- ☐ 1 pinch dried oregano leaves
- ☐ 2 cups chicken stock

Directions:
1. Cut the pork from the bone into large pieces and trim excess fat.
2. Set the pressure cooker to "Sauté" and heat the ghee. Place one layer of pork chunks into the pressure cooker and sauté for a few minutes, until they turn slightly brown.
3. When the meat browns, transfer it to a large bowl and set aside.
4. Pour in some chicken stock into the pressure cooker and scrape the bottom with a metal spatula. Place another layer of the pork into the pressure cooker and repeat the process until all the pork is browned. Then, add the chopped garlic, salt, pepper, garlic powder and oregano leaves.

5. Pour in 2 cups of chicken stock. Bring everything to a simmer.
6. Add all of the meat back in and stir well.
7. Seal the lid and set the cooking time to 42 minutes at high pressure.
8. When done, release the pressure naturally.
9. Open the lid and transfer the meat to a bowl. Pour over some of the broth.
10. Save the extra broth for later use.

Chicken Bone Broth

Prep Time: 15 minutes; **Cook Time:** 35 minutes

Pressure Level: High; **Release Type:** Natural

Serving Size: 269g; **Serves:** 8; **Calories:** 451

Total Fat: 26.9g **Saturated Fat:** 7.6g; **Trans Fat:** 0g

Protein: 39.1g; **Net Carbs:** 11g

Total Carbs: 12.8g; **Dietary Fiber:** 1.8g; **Sugars:** 6.1g

Cholesterol: 181mg; **Sodium:** 199mg; **Potassium:** 140mg;

Vitamin A: 77%; **Vitamin C:** 15%; **Calcium:** 7%; **Iron:** 13%.

Ingredients:
- 3.8 pounds whole chicken
- 2 medium carrots, cubed
- 2 ½ cups daikon radish, cubed
- 1 cup shiitake mushrooms, sliced
- 3 tablespoons goji berries, optional
- 4 large medjool dates
- 2 tea leaf bags mixed variety of Chinese dry herbal ingredients (ginseng, astragalus root)

Directions:
1. Rinse the chicken, pat it dry and trim any extra fat.
2. Put the whole chicken into the pressure cooker, along with the remaining ingredients.
3. Fill the pressure cooker with water up to the 3.5 qt. mark.
4. Press the "Soup" button and set the timer to 35 minutes at high pressure.
5. When done, release the pressure naturally.

Dinner
Indian Curry Lamb Spareribs

Prep Time: 10 minutes; **Cook Time:** 20 minutes

Pressure Level: High; **Release Type:** Natural

Serving Size: 413g; **Serves:** 4; **Calories:** 541

Total Fat: 28.8g **Saturated Fat:** 11.8g; **Trans Fat:** 0g

Protein: 58.8g; **Net Carbs:** 6.1g

Total Carbs: 8.2g; **Dietary Fiber:** 2.1g; **Sugars:** 1.9g

Cholesterol: 187mg; **Sodium:** 1093mg; **Potassium:** 293mg;

Vitamin A: 18%; **Vitamin C:** 40%; **Calcium:** 8%; **Iron:** 36%.

Ingredients:
Lamb
- ☐ 2.5 pounds pastured lamb spare ribs
- ☐ 2 teaspoons sea salt
- ☐ 1 tablespoons curry powder

Sauce
- ☐ 1 tablespoon coconut oil
- ☐ 1 large yellow onion, coarsely chopped
- ☐ ½ pound ripe tomatoes
- ☐ 5 cloves garlic, minced
- ☐ 1 tablespoon curry powder
- ☐ 1 teaspoon sea salt
- ☐ juice from 1 lemon
- ☐ 1 ¼ cup chopped cilantro, divided
- ☐ 4 scallions, thinly sliced

Directions:
1. Coat the spare ribs with salt and curry powder. Cover and place in the fridge for at least 4 hours.
2. Set the pressure cooker to "Sauté", heat the coconut oil and toss in the ribs. Brown the ribs and set them aside when done.

3. In the meantime, toss the onion and tomatoes into a blender and process until smooth.
4. Place the mixture into the pressure cooker and stir the garlic for about 30 seconds. Then add the tomato and onion mixture.
5. Add the curry powder, salt, lemon juice and cilantro. Bring everything to a boil and add the ribs back in. Stir well.
6. Seal the lid and cook at high pressure for 20 minutes.
7. When done, release the pressure naturally.
8. Stir in the scallions before servings.

Zucchini and Tomato Mélange

Prep Time: 10 minutes; **Cook Time:** 5 minutes

Pressure Level: High; **Release Type:** Natural

Serving Size: 469g; **Serves:** 4; **Calories:** 122

Total Fat: 4.1g **Saturated Fat:** 0.6g; **Trans Fat:** 0g

Protein: 5.2g; **Net Carbs:** 14.8g

Total Carbs: 20.2g; **Dietary Fiber:** 5.4g; **Sugars:** 10.3g

Cholesterol: 0mg; **Sodium:** 434mg; **Potassium:** 861mg;

Vitamin A: 24%; **Vitamin C:** 134%; **Calcium:** 8%; **Iron:** 11%.

Ingredients:
- 2 medium onions, roughly chopped
- 1 tablespoon olive oil
- 6 medium zucchini, roughly chopped
- 1 pound cherry tomatoes
- 1 cup water
- 1 teaspoon salt
- 2 garlic cloves, minced
- 1 bunch of basil

Directions:
1. Set the pressure cooker to "Sauté" and heat the olive oil. Toss in the chopped onions and sauté for about 5 minutes.
2. Then add the chopped zucchini, cherry tomatoes, water and salt. Seal the lid and cook on high for 5 minutes.
3. When done, release the pressure naturally. Stir in the minced garlic, strain out the vegetables and serve topped with fresh basil.
4. Keep the cooking liquid as vegetable stock for future use.

Green Chili with Chicken

Prep Time: 10 minutes; **Cook Time:** 15 minutes

Pressure Level: High; **Release Type:** Natural

Serving Size: 207g; **Serves**: 12; **Calories:** 368

Total Fat: 20.3g **Saturated Fat:** 5.2g; **Trans Fat:** 0g

Protein: 25.5g; **Net Carbs:** 15.2g

Total Carbs: 24.1g; **Dietary Fiber:** 8.9g; **Sugars:** 0.9g

Cholesterol: 95mg; **Sodium:** 245mg; **Potassium:** 1009mg;

Vitamin A: 157%; **Vitamin C:** 14%; **Calcium:** 5%; **Iron:** 29%.

Ingredients:
- [ ] 3 pounds bone-in skin-on chicken thighs and drumsticks
- [ ] ¾ pound tomatillos, quartered
- [ ] 1 pound poblano peppers, roughly chopped
- [ ] 6 ounces Anaheim or Cubanelle peppers, roughly chopped
- [ ] 2 Serrano or jalapeño chilies, roughly chopped
- [ ] 1 medium white onion, roughly chopped
- [ ] 6 cloves garlic, peeled
- [ ] sea salt, to taste
- [ ] ½ cup fresh cilantro leaves
- [ ] 1 tablespoon Asian fish sauce
- [ ] fresh corn tortillas and lime wedges, for serving

Directions:
1. Place the chicken, tomatillos, poblano peppers, Anaheim peppers, Serrano peppers, onion and garlic into the pressure cooker. Set it to "Sauté".
2. Heat until it starts to sizzle, then seal the lid.
3. Cook for 15 minutes at high pressure.
4. When done, release the pressure naturally.
5. Transfer the chicken to a separate bowl and set aside.
6. Place the cilantro leaves and fish sauce into the pressure cooker and blend everything using a hand blender. Season with salt.

7. Place the chicken back into the sauce and stir well.
8. Serve on individual plates with tortillas and lime.

Mexican Beef

Prep Time: 10 minutes; **Cook Time:** 35 minutes

Pressure Level: High; **Release Type:** Natural

Serving Size: 191g; **Serves:** 8; **Calories:** 580

Total Fat: 52.8g **Saturated Fat:** 23.5g; **Trans Fat:** 0g

Protein: 21.1g; **Net Carbs:** 2.8g

Total Carbs: 3.4g; **Dietary Fiber:** 0.6g; **Sugars:** 1.6g

Cholesterol: 111mg; **Sodium:** 467mg; **Potassium:** 99mg;

Vitamin A: 2%; **Vitamin C:** 6%; **Calcium:** 3%; **Iron:** 13%.

Ingredients:
- ☐ 2 ½ pounds boneless beef short ribs
- ☐ 1 tablespoon chili powder
- ☐ 1 ½ teaspoons sea salt
- ☐ 1 tablespoon ghee
- ☐ 1 red onion, sliced
- ☐ 6 garlic cloves, minced
- ☐ ½ cup homemade tomato salsa
- ☐ ½ cup bone broth
- ☐ black pepper, to taste

Directions:
1. Coat the beef with chili powder and salt.
2. Set the pressure cooker to "Sauté", heat the ghee and toss in the onion. Sauté until translucent.
3. Add in the garlic and cook for 30 seconds.
4. Then add the seasoned beef, tomato salsa and bone broth.
5. Seal the lid and press the "Keep Warm/Cancel" button on the pressure cooker.
6. Press the "Meat/Stew" button to start cooking. Cook at high pressure for 35 minutes.
7. When done, release the pressure naturally.
8. Season with freshly ground black pepper and serve.
9. Alternatively, you can store the dish in the refrigerator for up to 4 days.

Thai Beef Curry

Prep Time: 15 minutes; **Cook Time:** 35 minutes

Pressure Level: High; **Release Type:** Natural

Serving Size: 240g; **Serves:** 8; **Calories:** 524

Total Fat: 39.3g **Saturated Fat:** 16.4g; **Trans Fat:** 0g

Protein: 32.5g; **Net Carbs:** 8.3g

Total Carbs: 10.1g; **Dietary Fiber:** 1.8g; **Sugars:** 4g

Cholesterol: 134mg; **Sodium:** 805mg; **Potassium:** 219mg;

Vitamin A: 62%; **Vitamin C:** 22%; **Calcium:** 4%; **Iron:** 21%.

Ingredients:
- 3 pounds beef brisket, cubed
- 2 teaspoons sea salt
- 1 tablespoon coconut oil
- 2 tablespoons Thai curry paste
- 1 ½ cup full-fat coconut milk
- 2 tablespoons coconut aminos
- 1 tablespoon fish sauce
- 2 medium sweet potatoes, peeled and cubed
- 2 small onions, chopped
- 2 large carrots, peeled and chopped

Directions:
1. Rub the cubed beef with salt and toss it in a large bowl.
2. Set the pressure cooker to "Sauté" and heat the coconut oil. Add the curry paste and stir well.
3. Add the coconut milk, aminos and fish sauce. Stir well.
4. Toss in the beef cubes, sweet potatoes, onions and carrots.
5. Seal the lid and press the "Meat" button. This will let it cook for 35 minutes at high pressure.
6. When done, release the pressure naturally.
7. Ladle the stew into individual bowls and serve warm.

Summer Italian Chicken

Prep Time: 10 minutes; **Cook Time:** 10 minutes

Pressure Level: High; **Release Type:** Natural

Serving Size: 325g; **Serves:** 6; **Calories:** 289

Total Fat: 16.8g **Saturated Fat:** 4.3g; **Trans Fat:** 0g

Protein: 27.5g; **Net Carbs:** 7.4g

Total Carbs: 9.1g; **Dietary Fiber:** 1.7g; **Sugars:** 4.3g

Cholesterol: 120mg; **Sodium:** 285mg; **Potassium:** 495mg;

Vitamin A: 84%; **Vitamin C:** 41%; **Calcium:** 6%; **Iron:** 9%.

Ingredients:
- 8 boneless skinless boneless chicken thighs
- sea salt, to taste
- 1 tablespoon olive oil
- 1 small onion, chopped
- 2 medium carrots, chopped
- ½ pound cremini mushrooms, stemmed and quartered
- 3 garlic cloves, minced
- 2 cups cherry tomatoes
- ½ cup pitted green olives
- ½ cup loosely-packed fresh basil leaves, chopped
- ¼ cup loosely-packed fresh parsley, chopped

Directions:
1. Rub the chicken thighs with salt.
2. Set the pressure cooker to "Sauté" and heat the olive oil.
3. Toss in the onion, chopped carrots and mushrooms.
4. Sauté for about 3 to 5 minutes. Add the garlic and cook for 30 seconds more.
5. Toss in the chicken thighs, cherry tomatoes and green olives.
6. Stir well and seal the lid.
7. Cook for 10 minutes at high pressure.
8. When done, release the pressure naturally.

9. Open the lid and stir in fresh basil leaves and parsley. Serve warm.

Mexican Meatloaf

Prep Time: 10 minutes; **Cook Time:** 35 minutes

Pressure Level: High; **Release Type:** Natural

Serving Size: 235g; **Serves:** 6; **Calories:** 271

Total Fat: 15.3g **Saturated Fat:** 6g; **Trans Fat:** 0g

Protein: 30.3g; **Net Carbs:** 4.5g

Total Carbs: 5.8g; **Dietary Fiber:** 1.3g; **Sugars:** 2.5g

Cholesterol: 111mg; **Sodium:** 628mg; **Potassium:** 199mg;

Vitamin A: 3%; **Vitamin C:** 4%; **Calcium:** 2%; **Iron:** 29%.

Ingredients:
- [ ] 2 pounds ground beef
- [ ] 1 cup homemade tomato salsa
- [ ] 1 teaspoon cumin
- [ ] 1 teaspoon garlic powder
- [ ] 1 teaspoon paprika
- [ ] 1 teaspoon onion powder
- [ ] 1 teaspoon sea salt
- [ ] 1 large yellow onion, diced
- [ ] 1 egg
- [ ] ¼ cup almond flour
- [ ] 1 tablespoon olive oil

Directions:
1. In a large bowl, stir together all the ingredients, except for the olive oil.
2. Press the dough together firmly with your hands to form a loaf.
3. Set the pressure cooker to "Sauté" and heat the 1 tablespoon of olive oil.
4. Carefully transfer the meatloaf into the pressure cooker, seal the lid and set the pressure cooker to "Meat/Stew" function. Set the timer to 35 minutes and cook at high pressure.
5. When done, release the pressure naturally, open the lid and carefully remove the meatloaf.

Short Ribs

Prep Time: 30 minutes; **Cook Time:** 50 minutes

Pressure Level: High; **Release Type:** Natural

Serving Size: 415g; **Serves:** 4; **Calories:** 548

Total Fat: 26.2g **Saturated Fat:** 12.4g; **Trans Fat:** 0g

Protein: 37.4g; **Net Carbs:** 33.7g

Total Carbs: 36.3g; **Dietary Fiber:** 2.6g; **Sugars:** 22.9g

Cholesterol: 123mg; **Sodium:** 1561mg; **Potassium:** 116mg;

Vitamin A: 101%; **Vitamin C:** 12%; **Calcium:** 5%; **Iron:** 33%.

Ingredients:
- [ ] 2 tablespoons ghee
- [ ] 1-2 pounds short ribs, cut at the rib
- [ ] 1 onion, coarsely chopped
- [ ] 1 carrot, coarsely chopped
- [ ] 2 cloves garlic, minced
- [ ] 1 teaspoon dried thyme
- [ ] 1 teaspoon sea salt
- [ ] ½ teaspoon black pepper
- [ ] ¼ cup chicken stock
- [ ] 1 tablespoon maple syrup
- [ ] 2 cups chicken broth

Directions:
1. Set the pressure cooker to "Sauté" and heat the ghee. Toss in the short ribs and brown them for about 3 minutes per side. When done, remove from the pressure cooker and set aside.
2. Add the onion and carrot to the pressure cooker and sauté for about 5 minutes.
3. Toss in the garlic and sauté for 1 minute more. Season with thyme, salt, pepper, stock and maple syrup. Let it simmer until the liquid evaporates, then pour in the chicken broth.
4. Place the ribs back into the pressure cooker, stir well and seal the lid.

5. Press the "Meat" button and cook for 50 minutes.
6. When done, release the pressure naturally.
7. Open the lid and remove the ribs onto a plate. Set aside.
8. Transfer the liquid to a blender and blend until perfectly smooth.
9. Transfer it back into the pressure cooker and cook for about 5 more minutes, so the liquid evaporates by ¼.
10. Ladle the stew into individual bowls and place the ribs on top. Serve warm.

Chicken Sausage Stew

Prep Time: 15 minutes; **Cook Time:** 10 minutes

Pressure Level: High; **Release Type:** Natural

Serving Size: 482g; **Serves:** 6; **Calories:** 446

Total Fat: 27.6g **Saturated Fat:** 8.9g; **Trans Fat:** 0g

Protein: 32.6g; **Net Carbs:** 13.3g

Total Carbs: 17.6g; **Dietary Fiber:** 4.3g; **Sugars:** 5.8g

Cholesterol: 128mg; **Sodium:** 1199mg; **Potassium:** 838mg;

Vitamin A: 74%; **Vitamin C:** 196%; **Calcium:** 3%; **Iron:** 26%.

Ingredients:
- ☐ 1 pound boneless, skinless chicken thighs
- ☐ 1 pound andouille pork sausage
- ☐ 1 tablespoon coconut oil
- ☐ 1 medium white onion, chopped
- ☐ 2 stalks celery
- ☐ 3 bell peppers, diced
- ☐ 2 large carrots, diced
- ☐ 2 cups broth or water
- ☐ 6 cloves garlic, minced
- ☐ 6 cups tomatoes, chopped
- ☐ ¼ cup parsley
- ☐ 1 teaspoon sea salt
- ☐ ½ teaspoon crushed red chili flakes
- ☐ ¼ teaspoon black pepper
- ☐ ¼ teaspoon cayenne
- ☐ 1 bay leaf

Directions:
1. Set the pressure cooker to "Sauté", heat the oil and toss in the chicken and sausage. Let it cook for a few minutes.
2. Remove the meat and set it aside. Toss in the onion, celery, peppers and carrots and sauté until they turn brown.

3. Add the minced garlic, broth and chopped tomatoes. Bring everything to a simmer.
4. In the meantime, slice the chicken and sausage into small, bite-size pieces. Toss them back into the pot, along with parsley, salt, chili flakes, pepper, cayenne and bay leaf.
5. Seal the lid of the pressure cooker and cook for 5 to 10 minutes.
6. Remove the bay leaf when done and serve warm.

Pulled Pork Ragu

Prep Time: 10 minutes; **Cook Time:** 45 minutes

Pressure Level: High; **Release Type:** Natural

Serving Size: 367g; **Serves:** 4; **Calories:** 313

Total Fat: 5.7g **Saturated Fat:** 1.6g; **Trans Fat:** 0g

Protein: 36.2g; **Net Carbs:** 19.2g

Total Carbs: 25.8g; **Dietary Fiber:** 6.6g; **Sugars:** 14.7g

Cholesterol: 82mg; **Sodium:** 607mg; **Potassium:** 1073mg;

Vitamin A: 26%; **Vitamin C:** 21%; **Calcium:** 1%; **Iron:** 27%.

Ingredients:
- ☐ 1 pound pork tenderloin
- ☐ 1 teaspoon sea salt
- ☐ 1 teaspoon olive oil
- ☐ 5 cloves garlic, minced
- ☐ 1 (28-ounce) can crushed tomatoes
- ☐ 1 (7-ounce) jar roasted red peppers, drained
- ☐ 2 sprigs fresh thyme
- ☐ 2 bay leaves
- ☐ 1 tablespoon chopped fresh parsley, divided

Directions:
1. Season the pork with salt.
2. Set the pressure cooker to "Sauté", heat the olive oil and toss in the minced garlic. Sauté for about 1 to 2 minutes.
3. Add all the remaining ingredients and half of the fresh parsley.
4. Seal the lid and cook at high pressure for 45 minutes.
5. Release the pressure naturally, remove the bay leaves and shred the pork.
6. Sprinkle with the remaining parsley before serving.

Zucchini Pesto

Prep Time: 10 minutes; **Cook Time:** 3 minutes

Pressure Level: High; **Release Type:** Natural

Serving Size: 232g; **Serves:** 4; **Calories:** 79

Total Fat: 4.2g **Saturated Fat:** 0.6g; **Trans Fat:** 0g

Protein: 5g; **Net Carbs:** 5.9g

Total Carbs: 8.4g; **Dietary Fiber:** 2.5g; **Sugars:** 1.2g

Cholesterol: 0mg; **Sodium:** 7mg; **Potassium:** 826mg;

Vitamin A: 18%; **Vitamin C:** 100%; **Calcium:** 5%; **Iron:** 8%.

Ingredients:
- ☐ 1 tablespoon olive oil
- ☐ 1 onion, roughly chopped
- ☐ 1 ½ pounds zucchini, roughly chopped
- ☐ ½ cup water
- ☐ 1 teaspoons salt
- ☐ 1 bunch basil, leaves picked off
- ☐ 2 cloves garlic, minced

Directions:
1. Set the pressure cooker to "Sauté", heat the olive oil, add the chopped onion and sauté until it turns translucent.
2. Toss in the zucchini, water and salt. Seal the lid and cook for 3 minutes at high pressure.
3. When done, release the pressure naturally. Toss in the basil leaves and minced garlic and stir well.

Thai Chicken Breasts

Prep Time: 15 minutes; **Cook Time:** 10 minutes

Pressure Level: High; **Release Type:** Quick

Serving Size: 520g; **Serves:** 2; **Calories:** 363

Total Fat: 18.7g **Saturated Fat:** 10-7g; **Trans Fat:** 0g

Protein: 37.3g; **Net Carbs:** 10.3g

Total Carbs: 11.8g; **Dietary Fiber:** 1.5g; **Sugars:** 3.9g

Cholesterol: 123mg; **Sodium:** 1111mg; **Potassium:** 145mg;

Vitamin A: 3%; **Vitamin C:** 28%; **Calcium:** 4%; **Iron:** 1%.

Ingredients:
- ☐ 2 tablespoons ghee
- ☐ 1 inch fresh ginger, finely minced
- ☐ 4 cloves garlic, finely minced
- ☐ 1 medium red onion, thickly sliced
- ☐ 2 chicken breasts, diced
- ☐ juice of 1 lime
- ☐ 5-inch stem lemongrass, ends removed and halved
- ☐ 15 mint leaves
- ☐ 1 teaspoon sea salt
- ☐ ½ cup coconut milk
- ☐ ½ cup chicken bone broth
- ☐ ¼ cup coconut aminos

Directions:
1. Cut up the chicken and set it aside.
2. Set the pressure cooker to "Sauté" and heat the ghee. Toss in the minced ginger, garlic and red onion. Sauté for about 5 minutes.
3. Add the diced chicken breasts and cook for about 5 minutes, stirring occasionally. Turn the pressure cooker off by pressing "Cancel".
4. Add the lime juice, lemongrass, mint leaves, salt, coconut milk, bone broth and coconut aminos. Stir well.

5. Set the pressure cooker to "Poultry" and cook for 10 minutes.
6. When done, release the pressure quickly. Serve right away.

Simple Steamed Artichokes

Prep Time: 15 minutes; **Cook Time:** 10 minutes

Pressure Level: High; **Release Type:** Natural

Serving Size: 145g; **Serves:** 2; **Calories:** 160

Total Fat: 10.4g **Saturated Fat:** 1.5g; **Trans Fat:** 0g

Protein: 4.6g; **Net Carbs:** 42.1g

Total Carbs: 15.8g; **Dietary Fiber:** 7.9g; **Sugars:** 2g

Cholesterol: 5mg; **Sodium:** 229mg; **Potassium:** 518mg;

Vitamin A: 0%; **Vitamin C:** 41%; **Calcium:** 3%; **Iron:** 5%.

Ingredients:
- ☐ 2 medium artichokes
- ☐ 1 lemon, sliced in half
- ☐ 2 tablespoons mayonnaise
- ☐ 1 teaspoon Dijon mustard
- ☐ 1 pinch paprika

Directions:
1. Wash and trim the artichokes. Rub the cut edges with the lemon to prevent them from oxidizing.
2. Pour 1 to 2 cups of water into the pressure cooker base and set the steamer basket in its place.
3. Place the artichokes into the basket and drizzle them with lemon juice.
4. Seal the lid and cook for 10 minutes at high pressure.
5. When done, release the pressure naturally.
6. In a small bowl, mix the mayonnaise with mustard.
7. Serve the artichokes with the mustard mayonnaise mixture and sprinkle with paprika.

Simple Steamed Chicory

Prep Time: 10 minutes; **Cook Time:** 5 minutes

Pressure Level: High; **Release Type:** Natural

Serving Size: 180g; **Serves:** 2; **Calories:** 42

Total Fat: 0.5g **Saturated Fat:** 0.1g; **Trans Fat:** 0g

Protein: 3.1g; **Net Carbs:** 1.3g

Total Carbs: 8.5g; **Dietary Fiber:** 7.2g; **Sugars:** 1.3g

Cholesterol: 0mg; **Sodium:** 81mg; **Potassium:** 756mg;

Vitamin A: 206%; **Vitamin C:** 72%; **Calcium:** 18%; **Iron:** 9%.

Ingredients:
- 1-2 bunches chicory greens
- water

Directions:
1. Clean the chicory well and cut off the toughest parts of the stems.
2. Place the chicory into the pressure cooker and cover with water.
3. Seal the lid and cook at high pressure for 5 minutes.
4. When done, release the pressure naturally.
5. Drain the greens over a strainer and rinse them with cold water.
6. Serve as a side.

Pot Roast

Prep Time: 45 minutes; **Cook Time:** 45 minutes

Pressure Level: High; **Release Type:** Quick

Serving Size: 389g; **Serves:** 8; **Calories:** 509

Total Fat: 25.7g **Saturated Fat:** 12.2g; **Trans Fat:** 0g

Protein: 47.4g; **Net Carbs:** 19.8g

Total Carbs: 25.1g; **Dietary Fiber:** 5.3g; **Sugars:** 9.5g

Cholesterol: 129mg; **Sodium:** 384mg; **Potassium:** 694mg;

Vitamin A: 164%; **Vitamin C:** 51%; **Calcium:** 3%; **Iron:** 37%.

Ingredients:
- ☐ 3 pounds boneless chuck roast
- ☐ ½ teaspoon sea salt
- ☐ ¼ teaspoon black pepper
- ☐ 2 tablespoon ghee
- ☐ 1 small yellow onion, chopped
- ☐ 1 clove garlic, minced
- ☐ 1 tablespoon tomato paste
- ☐ 1 cup beef broth
- ☐ 1 cup chicken broth
- ☐ ¼ cup red wine
- ☐ 1 ½ pounds sweet potatoes, diced
- ☐ 1 pound carrots, chopped
- ☐ 8 ounces white mushrooms, halved

Directions:
1. Rub the roast with salt and pepper.
2. Set the pressure cooker to "Sauté", heat the ghee and add in the roast. Brown for about 6 minutes per side. Remove it from the pressure cooker and set aside.
3. Toss in the chopped onion and sauté for about 4 minutes, stirring frequently. Add in the garlic and tomato paste. Cook for another 30 seconds. Pour in the broths and wine. Stir well and bring to a simmer.
4. Seal the lid and press the "Stew/Meat" button. Set the timer to 45 minutes at high pressure.

5. When done, allow it to "Keep Warm" for 10 minutes, then release the pressure quickly.
6. Transfer the roast to a baking sheet and set aside.
7. Toss the diced sweet potatoes, carrots and mushrooms into the pressure cooker. Seal the lid and press the "Stew/Meat" button. Let it cook at high pressure for 6 minutes.
8. In the meantime, place the baking sheet with the roast into the oven and broil for about 4 minutes.
9. When the vegetables are done, release the pressure quickly. Transfer them to a baking sheet.
10. Set the pressure cooker to "Sauté" and let the liquid simmer until it is reduced to half.
11. Place the baking sheet back into the oven and broil for 5 minutes.
12. Slice the roast and transfer it to a platter, along with the vegetables. When thickened, pour the sauce over the roast and the vegetables.
13. Serve right away.

Goulash

Prep Time: 20 minutes; **Cook Time:** 40 minutes

Pressure Level: High; **Release Type:** Natural

Serving Size: 337g; **Serves:** 6; **Calories:** 345

Total Fat: 15.4g **Saturated Fat:** 7.1g; **Trans Fat:** 0g

Protein: 42.4g; **Net Carbs:** 8.7g

Total Carbs: 10.2g; **Dietary Fiber:** 1.5g; **Sugars:** 6g

Cholesterol: 106mg; **Sodium:** 305mg; **Potassium:** 670mg;

Vitamin A: 4%; **Vitamin C:** 81%; **Calcium:** 5%; **Iron:** 19%.

Ingredients:
- 2 teaspoons coconut oil
- 2 pounds diced beef
- 1 large onion, thinly sliced
- 1 red pepper, thinly sliced
- 1 green pepper, thinly sliced
- 1 yellow pepper, thinly sliced
- 3 cloves garlic, crushed
- 3 tablespoons paprika
- 1 pound passata
- 2 tablespoons tomato paste
- ½ cup beef stock
- sea salt and pepper, to taste
- 2 tablespoons chopped fresh parsley

Sour coconut cream
- ½ cup coconut milk or coconut cream
- 2 tablespoons lemon juice

Directions:
1. Set the pressure cooker to "Sauté", heat 1 tablespoon of oil and fry the meat in small batches.
2. Transfer the browned meat from the pressure cooker, add in 1 tablespoon of oil and sauté the onion and peppers until they soften.

3. Place the meat, along with the crushed garlic, back into the pressure cooker and sprinkle with paprika.
4. Add in the passata, tomato paste and beef stock. Seal the lid and press the "Meat" button. Set the timer to 40 minutes.
5. When done, release the pressure naturally.
6. Open the lid and stir in the chopped parsley. Season with salt and pepper.
7. Prepare the sour cream by whisking together the coconut cream and lemon juice.
8. Serve the goulash topped with sour cream.

Stuffed Cabbage Rolls

Prep Time: 30 minutes; **Cook Time:** 18 minutes

Pressure Level: High; **Release Type:** Quick

Serving Size: 248g; **Serves:** 15; **Calories:** 206

Total Fat: 8.9g **Saturated Fat:** 4.1g; **Trans Fat:** 0g

Protein: 19.5g; **Net Carbs:** 7.4g

Total Carbs: 10.9g; **Dietary Fiber:** 3.5g; **Sugars:** 5.7g

Cholesterol: 73mg; **Sodium:** 496mg; **Potassium:** 424mg;

Vitamin A: 8%; **Vitamin C:** 61%; **Calcium:** 4%; **Iron:** 14%.

Ingredients:
- 1 head cabbage
- 1 large egg
- 1 cup chopped onion
- 4 cloves garlic, minced
- 1 ½ teaspoon salt
- ½ teaspoon black pepper
- 1 ½ pounds lean ground beef
- ¾ pound ground pork

Sauce
- 2 tablespoons ghee
- 1 cup finely chopped onion
- 3 cloves garlic, minced
- 2 (14-ounce) cans diced tomatoes, with juice
- 1 (8-ounce) can tomato sauce
- ¼ cup white vinegar
- 2 teaspoons low sodium instant beef bouillon
- 1 teaspoon onion powder
- 3 dashes Paleo Worcestershire sauce
- 1 tablespoon almond flour
- 2 tablespoons cold water

Directions:
1. Fill a large pot half full with water. Bring to a boil.

2. Remove the core from the cabbage and place it into the boiling water. Cover with a lid and let it simmer for 7 to 8 minutes.
3. Remove the soft outer cabbage leaves and transfer them to a plate. Place the lid back on and cook for another 6 to 8 minutes. Again, remove the softened leaves to the plate to cool off. Repeat until you get to the center of the cabbage. When the leaves are too small for rolls, let the cabbage cook until crisp-tender. Remove the cabbage center from water, drain, coarsely chop and set aside.
4. Prepare the sauce by melting the ghee in a saucepan. Toss in the onion and cook until it turns translucent. Add the minced garlic and cook for another minute. Toss in the tomatoes, tomato sauce, white vinegar, bouillon, onion powder and Paleo Worcestershire sauce. Stir well.
5. Remove from heat and stir in the chopped cooked cabbage.
6. To prepare the filling, beat the egg with the onion, minced garlic, salt and pepper. Slowly knead in the ground beef and pork by hand.
7. Place one cabbage leaf onto your work surface, the stem end facing you. Put two tablespoons of the filling to the bottom of the leaf. Fold in the two sides and roll from the stem away from you. If you find it necessary, secure the finished roll with a toothpick to prevent it from falling apart.
8. Repeat the procedure with all the filling.
9. Pour 1 to 2 cups of water into the inner pot of the pressure cooker. Set the rack in its place and place 7 to 8 rolls onto the rack. Pour 1/3 of the sauce over them. Then, add another layer of rolls in the alternate direction. Cover with the rest of the sauce.
10. Seal the lid and cook for 18 minutes at high pressure.
11. When done, wait for 15 minutes, then release the pressure quickly.
12. Transfer the rolls to a plate and set aside.
13. Set the pressure cooker to "Sauté" and bring the remaining sauce to a simmer.

14. Whisk together the almond flour and water in a small bowl. Pour the mixture into the sauce and stir until it thickens.
15. Serve the rolls with the sauce.

Smoked Sausage Stew

Prep Time: 15 minutes; **Cook Time:** 10 minutes

Pressure Level: High; **Release Type:** Natural

Serving Size: 530g; **Serves**: 6; **Calories:** 447

Total Fat: 26.7g **Saturated Fat**: 8.9g; **Trans Fat**: 0g

Protein: 34.8g; **Net Carbs:** 11.9g

Total Carbs: 16.3g; **Dietary Fiber:** 4.4g; **Sugars:** 8.2g

Cholesterol: 126mg; **Sodium**: 953mg; **Potassium**: 904mg;

Vitamin A: 104%; **Vitamin C**: 208%; **Calcium**: 5%; **Iron**: 25%.

Ingredients:
- 1 pound boneless, skinless chicken thighs
- 1 pound andouille pork sausage
- 1 tablespoon coconut oil
- 1 medium white onion, sliced
- 2 stalks celery, chopped
- 3 bell peppers, diced
- 2 large carrots, chopped
- 6 cloves garlic, minced
- 6 cups chopped tomatoes
- 2 cups bone broth
- ¼ cup parsley, minced
- 1 teaspoon salt
- 1 teaspoon thyme
- ½ teaspoon crushed red chili flakes
- ¼ teaspoon black pepper
- 1 bay leaf

Directions:
1. Set the pressure cooker to "Sauté", heat the oil and toss in the chicken and sausage. Cook until browned on all sides.
2. Transfer the meat from the pressure cooker and set aside.

3. Toss the onion, celery, peppers and carrots into the pressure cooker and sauté for a few minutes. Add the garlic and sauté for another minute.
4. Pour in the bone broth and add the chopped tomatoes. Bring everything to a simmer.
5. In the meantime, cut the meat into bite-size pieces. Transfer them back to the pressure cooker, along with minced parsley, salt, thyme, red chili flakes, pepper and bay leaf.
6. Press the "Soup" button and let it cook for 5 to 10 minutes.
7. When done, release the pressure naturally.
8. Serve warm.

Desserts and Snacks
Mini Pumpkin Pies

Prep Time: 20 minutes; **Cook Time:** 10 minutes

Pressure Level: High; **Release Type:** Natural

Serving Size: 179g; **Serves:** 8; **Calories:** 152

Total Fat: 1.6g **Saturated Fat:** 0.4g; **Trans Fat:** 0g

Protein: 2.8g; **Net Carbs:** 32g

Total Carbs: 34.4g; **Dietary Fiber:** 2.4g; **Sugars:** 22.5g

Cholesterol: 46mg; **Sodium:** 61mg; **Potassium:** 433mg;

Vitamin A: 242%; **Vitamin C:** 39%; **Calcium:** 14%; **Iron:** 9%.

Ingredients:
- 2 pounds butternut squash, peeled and diced
- 1 cup almond milk
- ¾ cup maple syrup
- 2 large eggs
- 1 teaspoon cinnamon
- ½ teaspoon ginger
- 1 tablespoon almond flour
- 1 pinch sea salt

Directions:
1. Pour 1 to 2 cups of water into the pressure cooker base.
2. Set the steamer basket in its place and add in the diced butternut squash.
3. Seal the lid and cook for 4 minutes at high pressure.
4. Meanwhile, beat together the almond milk, maple syrup, eggs, cinnamon, ginger, almond flour and salt in a large bowl.
5. Release the pressure quickly.
6. Transfer the butternut squash into a bowl and, once cooled, press it with a fine-mesh strainer to release the liquid.
7. Measure 2 cups of the strained butternut squash and save the rest for later use.

8. Add 2 cups of butternut squash into the egg mixture and blend.
9. Pour 1 to 2 cups of water into the pressure cooker base and set the trivet or steamer basket in its place.
10. Pour the butternut squash mixture into individual ramekins and place them into the pressure cooker.
11. Seal the lid and cook for 10 minutes at high pressure.
12. When done, release the pressure naturally.
13. Remove the pies from the pressure cooker and let them chill for at least 5 minutes before serving. Store covered in the fridge for up to 2 days.

Paleo Banana Bread

Prep Time: 20 minutes; **Cook Time:** 30 minutes

Pressure Level: High; **Release Type:** Natural

Serving Size: 100g; **Serves:** 8; **Calories:** 220

Total Fat: 5.7g **Saturated Fat:** 2.4g; **Trans Fat:** 0g

Protein: 1.2g; **Net Carbs:** 40.3g

Total Carbs: 42.5g; **Dietary Fiber:** 2.2g; **Sugars:** 22.4g

Cholesterol: 29mg; **Sodium:** 128mg; **Potassium**: 121mg;

Vitamin A: 1%; **Vitamin C:** 4%; **Calcium**: 4%; **Iron**: 3%.

Ingredients:
- ☐ 1/3 cup almond milk
- ☐ 1 ½ teaspoon cream of tartar
- ☐ 1/3 cup softened ghee
- ☐ ¾ cup coconut sugar
- ☐ 1 egg
- ☐ 1 teaspoon vanilla
- ☐ 2 mashed bananas
- ☐ 1 ½ cup almond flour
- ☐ 1 teaspoon baking soda

Directions:
1. In a small bowl, mix together the almond milk and cream of tartar. Set aside.
2. Beat together the ghee and coconut sugar. Add the egg and vanilla. Stir well.
3. Add the mashed bananas and continue stirring.
4. In a medium bowl, mix together the almond flour and baking soda. Slowly pour into the wet ingredients while stirring constantly.
5. Pour in the milk mixture and stir.
6. Pour the batter into a greased 7-inch cake pan and cover it with foil.
7. Add 2 cups of water into the pressure cooker and set the metal trivet rack to the bottom of the pressure cooker

8. Place the cake pan onto the trivet.
9. Seal the lid and press "Manual" to 30 minutes.
10. When done, release the pressure naturally. Remove the pan from the cooker, remove the foil and let it cool off on a wire rack while still in the pan.

Strawberry Rhubarb Compote

Prep Time: 10 minutes; **Cook Time:** 2 minutes

Pressure Level: High; **Release Type:** Natural

Serving Size: 303g; **Serves:** 3; **Calories:** 160

Total Fat: 0.7g **Saturated Fat:** 0.1g; **Trans Fat:** 0g

Protein: 2.2g; **Net Carbs:** 35.2g

Total Carbs: 40.5g; **Dietary Fiber:** 5.3g; **Sugars:** 32g

Cholesterol: 0mg; **Sodium:** 8mg; **Potassium:** 598mg;

Vitamin A: 3%; **Vitamin C:** 164%; **Calcium:** 13%; **Iron:** 6%.

Ingredients:
- 3 cups sliced rhubarb
- 1 pound strawberries, quartered
- ¼ cup water
- 1 teaspoon lemon zest
- 1 teaspoon fresh lemon juice
- ¼ cup honey

Directions:
1. Put the sliced rhubarb, quartered strawberries and water into the pressure cooker.
2. Seal the lid, press "Manual" and set to 2 minutes.
3. When done, release the pressure naturally.
4. Open the lid and add in the lemon zest, lemon juice and honey.
5. Set the pressure cooker to "Sauté" and let the mixture simmer until the compote is thickened to your liking.

Blueberry Jam

Prep Time: 10 minutes; **Cook Time:** 2 minutes	
Pressure Level: High; **Release Type:** Natural	
Serving Size: 112g; **Serves:** 12; **Calories:** 152	
Total Fat: 0.5g **Saturated Fat:** 0g; **Trans Fat:** 0g	
Protein: 0.4g; **Net Carbs:** 37.9g	
Total Carbs: 40g; **Dietary Fiber:** 2.1g; **Sugars:** 37.1g	
Cholesterol: 0mg; **Sodium:** 2mg; **Potassium:** 60mg;	
Vitamin A: 1%; **Vitamin C:** 4%; **Calcium:** 1%; **Iron:** 2%.	

Ingredients:
- [ ] 2 pounds blueberries, fresh or frozen
- [ ] 1 pound honey

Directions:
1. Place the blueberries and honey into the pressure cooker.
2. Set the "Keep Warm" function until the honey melts. Stir occasionally.
3. When melted, set the pressure to "Sauté" until the mixture boils.
4. Once boiling, cover and seal the lid and set the timer to 2 minutes at high pressure.
5. When done, press the "Cancel" button and let the pressure release naturally.
6. Remove the lid and set the pressure cooker back to "Sauté".
7. Let it boil until the jam thickens to your desired consistency. Stir frequently.
8. Store the cooked jam in half-pint jars in the fridge.

Apple Pie Applesauce

Prep Time: 10 minutes; **Cook Time:** 5 minutes

Pressure Level: High; **Release Type:** Natural

Serving Size: 533g; **Serves:** 3; **Calories:** 304

Total Fat: 3.3g **Saturated Fat:** 2g; **Trans Fat:** 0g

Protein: 0g; **Net Carbs:** 58.4g

Total Carbs: 75.3g; **Dietary Fiber:** 16.9g; **Sugars:** 58.1g

Cholesterol: 7mg; **Sodium:** 1mg; **Potassium:** 679mg;

Vitamin A: 3%; **Vitamin C:** 192%; **Calcium:** 0%; **Iron:** 211%.

Ingredients:
- 3 ½ pounds apples (gala, granny smith and fuji), peeled and sliced
- ¾ cup water
- 2 teaspoons lemon juice
- 2 teaspoons ghee
- ¼ teaspoon ground cinnamon
- 1/8 teaspoon ground allspice

Directions:
1. Place the sliced apples, water, lemon juice, ghee, cinnamon and allspice into the pressure cooker.
2. Seal the lid and press "Manual". Cook at high pressure for 5 minutes.
3. When done, release the pressure naturally.
4. Transfer the contents into a blender or food processor and puree to your desired consistency.
5. Serve warm.

Poached Plums

Prep Time: 20 minutes; **Cook Time:** 15 minutes

Pressure Level: High; **Release Type:** Natural

Serving Size: 239g; **Serves:** 3; **Calories:** 179

Total Fat: 1.7g **Saturated Fat:** 0g; **Trans Fat:** 0g

Protein: 3.5g; **Net Carbs:** 42.2g

Total Carbs: 45.6g; **Dietary Fiber:** 3.4g; **Sugars:** 28.6g

Cholesterol: 0mg; **Sodium:** 1mg; **Potassium:** 382mg;

Vitamin A: 14%; **Vitamin C:** 34%; **Calcium:** 0%; **Iron:** 1%.

Ingredients:
- ☐ 1.5 pounds fresh plums, pitted and halved
- ☐ 1.5 cups water
- ☐ 1 vanilla bean pod, split and seeded
- ☐ 1 star anise
- ☐ 2 cinnamon sticks
- ☐ 4 cloves
- ☐ 3 cardamom pods
- ☐ 2 tablespoons honey

Directions:
1. Place the plums into the pressure cooker.
2. Scrape the vanilla seeds out of each vanilla pod half and save them for later use.
3. Pour water into the pressure cooker. Add the vanilla pod halves, anise, cinnamon, cloves, cardamom pods and honey.
4. Seal the lid and cook for 15 minutes at high pressure.
5. When done, release the pressure naturally.
6. Uncover the pressure cooker, remove the cooked plums and cook the liquid with the lid off until it is reduced by half.
7. Pour this syrup over the plums and serve warm.

Pumpkin Pudding

Prep Time: 15 minutes; **Cook Time:** 30 minutes

Pressure Level: High; **Release Type:** Quick

Serving Size: 96g; **Serves:** 5; **Calories:** 119

Total Fat: 1.4g **Saturated Fat:** 0.7g; **Trans Fat:** 0g

Protein: 1.9g; **Net Carbs:** 25.1g

Total Carbs: 26.1g; **Dietary Fiber:** 1g; **Sugars:** 23.8g

Cholesterol: 37mg; **Sodium:** 20mg; **Potassium:** 18mg;

Vitamin A: 86%; **Vitamin C:** 2%; **Calcium:** 3%; **Iron:** 2%.

Ingredients:
- ½ cup coconut milk
- 2 teaspoons gelatin
- ¾ cup packed pumpkin puree
- ½ cup coconut sugar
- 1 egg
- 1 teaspoon cinnamon
- ½ teaspoon nutmeg
- ½ teaspoon ginger
- ½ teaspoon allspice
- 1 cup water

Directions:
1. Pour the coconut milk into a saucepan and add the gelatin. On medium-low heat, slowly warm up the milk. Stir well, so the gelatin dissolves. Remove the saucepan from the heat.
2. Whisk together the gelatin milk, pumpkin puree, coconut sugar, egg, cinnamon, nutmeg, ginger and allspice.
3. Pour the mixture into a greased 3-cup bowl or soufflé dish.
4. Pour 1 cup of water into the pressure cooker and set the trivet in its place.
5. Place the dish with the pudding onto the trivet.

6. Seal the lid and set the pressure to high. Cook for 30 minutes.
7. When done, release the pressure quickly.
8. Place the pudding into the fridge and let it set for 4 to 6 hours.
9. When set, turn the pudding over onto a plate and serve.

Rosemary Apple Sauce

Prep Time: 15 minutes; **Cook Time:** 5 minutes	
Pressure Level: High; **Release Type:** Natural	
Serving Size: 286g; **Serves:** 5; **Calories:** 182	
Total Fat: 0g **Saturated Fat:** 0g; **Trans Fat:** 0g	
Protein: 0g; **Net Carbs:** 40.5g	
Total Carbs: 49.3g; **Dietary Fiber:** 8.8g; **Sugars:** 39.3g	
Cholesterol: 0mg; **Sodium:** 1mg; **Potassium:** 33mg;	
Vitamin A: 4%; **Vitamin C:** 35%; **Calcium:** 5%; **Iron:** 4%.	

Ingredients:
- ☐ 3 pounds apples, any variety
- ☐ 1 long sprig fresh rosemary
- ☐ ½ cup water
- ☐ 4 tablespoons maple syrup

Directions:
1. Peel, core and chop the apples.
2. Place the chopped apples, rosemary, water and maple syrup to the pressure cooker.
3. Seal the lid and set the pressure cooker to "Manual". Cook at high pressure for 5 minutes.
4. When done, release the pressure naturally.
5. Transfer the cooked apples to a blender and puree until perfectly smooth.
6. Serve as is or sprinkle with some cinnamon.

Baked Apples

Prep Time: 5 minutes; **Cook Time:** 10 minutes

Pressure Level: High; **Release Type:** Natural

Serving Size: 217g; **Serves:** 6; **Calories:** 202

Total Fat: 0g **Saturated Fat:** 0g; **Trans Fat:** 0g

Protein: 0.2g; **Net Carbs:** 41.3g

Total Carbs: 46.4g; **Dietary Fiber:** 5.1g; **Sugars:** 39.4g

Cholesterol: 0mg; **Sodium:** 2mg; **Potassium:** 296mg;

Vitamin A: 0%; **Vitamin C:** 55%; **Calcium:** 1%; **Iron:** 63%.

Ingredients:
- ☐ 6 apples, cored
- ☐ ¼ cup raisins
- ☐ 1 cup red wine
- ☐ ½ cup coconut sugar
- ☐ 1 teaspoon cinnamon powder

Directions:
1. Place the apples into the base of the pressure cooker. Pour in the red wine, add the raisins, coconut sugar and cinnamon.
2. Seal the lid and set the timer to 10 minutes at high pressure.
3. When done, release the pressure naturally.
4. Serve in individual serving bowls, along with the cooking liquid.

Cinnamon Poached Pears with Chocolate Sauce

Prep Time: 15 minutes; **Cook Time:** 3 minutes

Pressure Level: High; **Release Type:** Quick

Serving Size: 381g; **Serves:** 6; **Calories:** 678

Total Fat: 23.4g **Saturated Fat:** 16.2g; **Trans Fat:** 0g

Protein: 3.1g; **Net Carbs:** 91g

Total Carbs: 99.7g; **Dietary Fiber:** 8.7g; **Sugars:** 83.3g

Cholesterol: 6mg; **Sodium:** 8mg; **Potassium:** 283mg;

Vitamin A: 2%; **Vitamin C:** 12%; **Calcium:** 3%; **Iron:** 1%.

Ingredients:
- ☐ 1 lemon, halved
- ☐ 5 cups water
- ☐ 1 cup honey
- ☐ 6 cinnamon sticks
- ☐ 6 Bartlett pears

Chocolate sauce
- ☐ 9 ounces dark chocolate cut in ½-inch pieces
- ☐ ½ cup coconut milk
- ☐ ¼ cup coconut oil
- ☐ 2 tablespoons honey

Directions:
1. Place the water, honey, and cinnamon into the pressure cooker. Set it to "Sauté" and bring everything to a simmer, so the sugar dissolves. Switch to "Keep Warm".
2. Peel the pears and keep them whole, with the stems intact. Rub them with the lemon half to prevent browning.
3. Drop the pears into the syrup, seal the lid and cook for 3 minutes at high pressure.
4. When done, release the pressure quickly.

5. Remove the pears and pour the syrup, once cooled, over them.
6. Prepare the chocolate sauce. Put the dark chocolate into a bowl. In a saucepan, heat the milk, oil and honey. Pour the hot mixture over the chocolate and whish until perfectly smooth.
7. Place each pear onto an individual serving plate and pour the warm chocolate sauce over it.
8. Serve right away.

CPSIA information can be obtained
at www.ICGtesting.com
Printed in the USA
LVOW13s1501310817

547105LV00021B/643/P